Collins

Easy Learning

English

Age 6-7

My name is **Mia** .

I am **6** years old.

I go to .... School.

My favourite book is ....

Illustrated by Rachel Annie Bridgen

How to use this book

- Find a quiet, comfortable place to work, away from other distractions.
- Tackle one topic at a time.
- Help with reading the instructions where necessary, and ensure that your child understands what to do.
- Help and encourage your child to check their own answers as they complete each activity.
- Discuss with your child what they have learnt.
- Let your child return to their favourite pages once they have been completed, to talk about the activities.
- Reward your child with plenty of praise and encouragement.

Special features

- Parent's notes: These are divided into 'What you need to know', which explain the key English idea, and 'Taking it further', which suggest activities and encourage discussion with your child about what they have learnt. The words in bold are key words that you should focus on when talking to your child.

Published by Collins
An imprint of HarperCollins*Publishers*
77–85 Fulham Palace Road
Hammersmith
London
W6 8JB

Browse the complete Collins catalogue at www.collins.co.uk

© HarperCollins*Publishers* Limited 2006

10 9 8 7 6 5 4 3

ISBN-13 978-0-00-721024-4
ISBN-10 0-00-721024-8

All rights reserved. No part of this publication may be reproduced, stored in a retrieval system, or transmitted in any form or by any means, electronic, mechanical, photocopying, recording or otherwise, without the prior written permission of the Publisher or a licence permitting restricted copying in the United Kingdom issued by the Copyright Licensing Agency Ltd., 90 Tottenham Court Road, London W1T 4LP.

British Library Cataloguing in Publication Data
A Catalogue record for this publication is available from the British Library

Design and layout by Lodestone Publishing Limited, Uckfield, East Sussex; www.lodestonepublishing.com
Illustrated by Rachel Annie Bridgen; www.shootingthelight.com, and Kathy Baxendale
Printed and bound in China

Contents

How to use this book	2
Handwriting	4
Long vowel sounds	6
Magic e	8
Words ending with l and v sounds	10
Words ending with -ing and -ed	12
Same sound, different spelling	14
Word sums	16
Adjectives	18
Writing sentences	20
Joining sentences	22
Punctuation marks	24
Verb tenses	26
Reading non-fiction	28
Reading log	30
Answers	32

Handwriting

Practise the alphabet

- Write each letter as you are taught to write it at school.

a b c d e f g h i j k l m n o p q r s t u v w x y z

abcdefghijKLmnopqrsturwxyz ✓

- This sentence includes every letter of the alphabet. Copy it in joined writing, as you are taught to do joins at school.

The quick brown fox jumps over the lazy dog.

The quick brown Fox jumps over the lazy dog

Practise joins

- Use your best joined writing to write out this rhyme.

The quick brown fox says, 'Let's have a race!'

The quick brown Fox Says, 'Let's|

He gallops and jumps all over the place.

The lazy dog shakes his sleepy old head:

'I think I'll just have a snooze instead.'

What you need to know How to join letters in handwriting.
Even though we use computers so much now it will always be important to have neat, legible handwriting.

Alphabet sentence

- Make up your own sentence that includes every letter of the alphabet.
- Write it here in your best joined handwriting.

_____

Why does it matter?

- Finish these sentences.

I need good handwriting because

_____

The best thing about my handwriting is

_____

The worst thing about my handwriting is

_____

When I write in future I will try to

_____

Taking it further Encourage your child to practise neat handwriting on shopping lists, birthday cards, invitations and replies, postcards and letters.

Long vowel sounds

Long o sounds

When o comes next to other letters it makes different long vowel sounds: oa oe oi oo ou or ow oy

- Choose the right sound to finish these words.

 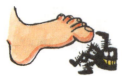  

b___ ___t   t___ ___   p___ ___nt   m___ ___n

m___ ___se   h___ ___se   ___ ___l   b___ ___

How do you say ow?

The **ow** sound can be said in two ways:

	ow as in owl	ow as in crow

- Write these **ow** words in the right lists.

window
snow
cow
blow
down
flower

What you need to know How to spell the different long **o** and long **e** vowel sounds. English spelling uses lots of different letter combinations to make all the long vowel sounds. Many of these just have to be learned!

Long e sounds

There are two ways of spelling the long e sound: **ee** or **ea**.

 green   peach

- Fill in the right spellings.

The tr____ ____ is gr____ ____n.

S____ ____ if you can s____ ____ the s____ ____!

Holly was stung by a b____ ____ at the b____ ____ch.

Little Jack Horner

- Fill in the right spellings in this rhyme.

Little Jack H____ ____ner

Sat in a c____ ____ner

____ ____ting a lump of ch____ ____se.

A tiny w____ ____ m____ ____se

Came ____ ____t of his h____ ____se

And said, 'Thr____ ____ me

a bit, pl____ ____se!'

Taking it further Collect words with different long vowel sounds. Make vowel 'trees' with different sounds and spellings for each branch, adding word examples, e.g. **ee** feet, three, teeth, **ea** peas, cream, squeak, etc.

Magic e

What does magic e do?

When you put a magic e on the end of a word, it changes the short vowel sound in the middle to a long vowel sound.

Use your magic wand!

- Use your wand to change these words into magic e words.
- Fill the gaps in the words under each picture.

p___ ___   p___ ___ ___   r___ ___   r___ ___ ___

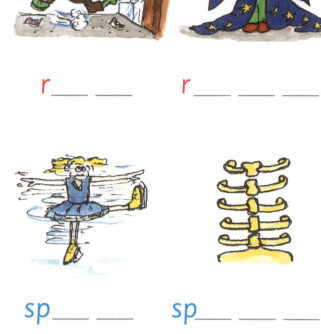

c___ ___   c___ ___ ___   sp___ ___   sp___ ___ ___

What you need to know How magic e changes short vowel sounds to long vowel sounds. This is a very important spelling rule!

More pairs

- Choose the best word to fill the gaps.

  hat**hate**

  You wear a _____ on your head.

  I love beans but I _____ peas!

  win**wine**

  I hope I _____ the race.

  Dad bought a bottle of _____.

  tub**tube**

  You get ice cream in a _____.

  You get toothpaste in a _____.

The magic e song

- Learn this magic e song, and sing it to the tune of The Wheels on the Bus.

  The e on the end makes
  came, game, same,
  time, lime, chime,
  bone, phone, stone
  The e on the end makes
  came, game, same
  All day long.

Taking it further Using magic e, make up more strings of rhyming words, and put them in the song.

Words ending with l and v sounds

Endings with –le

Most words that end with an **l** sound are spelt **-le**.

- Add **-le** to these word beginnings.
  Write the words under the pictures.

  ank   jugg   bott   cand   scribb   tab   pudd   need

_____   _____   _____   _____

_____   _____   _____   _____

Endings with –al

Just a few words that end with an **l** sound are spelt **-al**.

- Match these words to the pictures.

animal   petal   hospital

What you need to know   How to spell other tricky endings.
English spelling *is* difficult! The best way to learn spelling rules is to list all the words that follow a rule, and then list those that either break it, or make a different rule.

Endings with –ve

No English word ends in v, so you always write -ve on the end.

- Write these words under the pictures.

    hive   cave   save   glove

(And remember how to spell of, even though it sounds like ov!)

Find the –ve words

- There are eight -ve words in this letter.
  Write them next to the letter.

Dear e,
You have so many jobs to do on the ends of words. I don't know how you live with it! You slave away all day long and what do they give you? Just more work! I'm surprised you don't leave the country and move somewhere else.
   Love,
   Dave

Taking it further Collect rhyming words in each of these spelling groups: **-le, -al, -ve**. Make funny rhymes with them, or play I-spy, something that rhymes with … .

Words ending with –ing and –ed

Adding –ing

We add -ing to action words if they are happening now.
  I jump   I am jump**ing**

- Add -ing to these words. Write them under the pictures.

  watch   walk   lift   draw

_____ _____ _____ _____

Drop e and add –ing

If the word ends with **e**, you drop the **e** before you add **-ing**.

- Add -ing to these words.

make_____   take_____   come_____   live_____

have_____   use_____   write_____   excite_____

What you need to know   How to add **-ing** and **-ed** endings, and when they change the spelling of words.

Adding –ed

We add -ed to action words if they happened in the past.
   I jump   I jump**ed**

- Add -ed to these words. Write them under the pictures.

   climb   talk   listen   pull

_____   _____   _____   _____

Present or past?

- Fill the gaps with words using -ing for the present tense, or -ed for the past.

Now I am _____ my teeth.

In the past, I _____ my teeth.

In the past, I _____ TV.

Now I am _____ TV.

Taking it further Tell stories in the present, and then tell them again in the past. Which words change? Can your child write down the action verbs?

Same sound, different spelling

Hear or here?

These two words sound the same but mean different things.
You **hear** with your ear.   **Here** means in this place.

- Fill the gaps with the right spellings.

Can you ____ ____ ____ ____ the radio?

Come over ____ ____ ____ ____ !

I can't ____ ____ ____ ____ what you're saying.

Where's my bag? ____ ____ ____ ____ it is!

There or their?

There is a place: over there.
Their means belonging to them: their coats.

- Fill the gaps with the right spellings.

I live over ____ ____ ____ ____ ____ .

The twins put ____ ____ ____ ____ ____ toys away.

We played at ____ ____ ____ ____ ____ house all day.

____ ____ ____ ____ ____ is nobody here.

What you need to know Some words sound the same but are spelt differently. There are lots of tricky examples in English; the ones on these two pages are the most common.

To, two or too?

To is a short word we use a lot: to sing, go to play.
Two is the number 2.
And **too** means as well, or too much: too hot, me too.

- Fill the gaps with the right spellings.

It was _____ cold _____ go out.

The little girl is _____ years old.

We're going _____ a party.

Do you want _____ come _____ ?

Off or of?

These two words sound different.
   I fell **off** the wall (sounds like **f**).
   A box **of** chocolates (sounds like **v**).

- Fill the gaps with the right spellings.

I jumped _____ the wall.

Would you like a drink _____ lemonade?

We saw the King _____ Spain.

We turned the light _____ .

Taking it further All these words are very easy to get wrong.
If your child uses the wrong spelling, come back to these pages and practise them again.

Word sums

If you see a long word, break it down into chunks. This will help you to understand the meaning, and get the spelling right.

Football and superstore

- These words are made up of two separate words. Add them together to make a new meaning.

foot + ball
super + store

grand + father = _____

news + paper = _____

light + house = _____

tooth + brush = _____

The new words are all nouns.
Cat and dog are both nouns.
A noun is a word that names a thing or an object.

Thereabouts

Sometimes the separate parts of a word don't mean much, but it makes it easier to read if you break down the word.

- Break down these words into two smaller words.

everywhere = _____ + _____

sometimes = _____ + _____

grasshopper = _____ + _____

thereabouts = _____ + _____

What you need to know How to break long words down into parts. This usually helps to explain the meaning of the word. Or it will help you to find the **root** and its **ending** so you can spell the word correctly. This is also a good time to introduce the word **noun** for naming things.

Roots and endings

Remember what you learned about the endings -ed and -ing? The main word is called the root word. You can cut off the ending to help you spell the root word.

- Write the root word and the ending of these words.

drawing = _____ + _____

speaking = _____ + _____

explained = _____ + _____

learned = _____ + _____

Other endings

- Cut up these words into chunks. Do you know what each ending means?

singer = _____ + _____

actor = _____ + _____

yellowish = _____ + _____

lioness = _____ + _____

Taking it further Collect groups of words with **-er**, **-or**, **-ish** and **-ess** endings from story books you read together. You could write the whole words on bits of paper and then cut them up into chunks. How many endings can you add to each root word?

Adjectives

Adjectives are words that **describe** things.
    a **bouncy** cat   a **cuddly** cat
Using adjectives makes your writing more interesting.

Game

- Play this game with a friend.
- Go through the alphabet, and take it in turns think of an adjective for a cat.

My cat is an *angry* cat.

My cat is a *bouncy* cat
etc.

Same or different?

- Take each adjective from the game, and think of an adjective that means the same.
- Then think of one that means the opposite.

If you have a thesaurus or dictionary, look up adjectives which mean the same, or the opposite.

What you need to know How to use more and better adjectives to improve descriptions in writing.
Adjective is the second grammar term introduced after noun.

Adjectives and nouns

Adjectives are describing words.
Nouns are the things that the adjectives describe.

- In this picture there are four nouns and four adjectives.
  List them under the right headings.

sword   glittering

princess   monster

                                            cave

fearless

terrified   gloomy

Adjectives	Nouns

Write a story

- Use the adjectives and nouns from the picture to fill the gaps in this story.

The fierce monster jumped up at the _____,

so she took out her _____

_____ and waved it at him. With a cry of fear, the

_____

turned and fled into his _____.

Taking it further Collect more adjectives, and check in a dictionary or thesaurus for similar and opposite meanings.

Writing sentences

Sentences always start with a capital letter and end with a full stop.

Punctuation

- There are three sentences below. Read them aloud and mark where each one begins and ends.
- Then write them out with capital letters and full stops.

The seagull flew high in the sky it was making a screeching sound it then dived into the sea

_____

_____

_____

Game

- Play this game with a partner. One of you reads a story aloud. The other one bounces a ball each time they hear the end of a sentence.
- You could also call out 'Capital letter!' for the start of each new sentence.

What you need to know How to punctuate the beginning and end of sentences.
This is a good time to explain the word **punctuation**, which means the 'signposts' in sentences. You can also introduce the third grammar term, **verb** (the action word), which all sentences need in order to make sense.

Making sense

Sentences have to make complete sense before you add the punctuation.

This is not a sentence: a white bird in the sky

But this is a sentence: A white bird flew in the sky.

Which word makes the difference?
It's the action word, flew, which is called a verb.

Is there a verb?

- Copy these words under the right headings.

a big red ball   my name is Monty

the donkey ate a carrot   blue sky the beach sea

very slowly   the sun shines in summer

Sentences (include verbs)	Not sentences (no verbs)

- Now underline the verbs.
- Then add capital letters and full stops.

Taking it further Look at posters and adverts, and talk about which have complete sentences.

Joining sentences

Count the sentences

- How many sentences are there in these two stories?

1 I woke up. The sun was shining through the curtains. I put on jeans and a T-shirt instead of school clothes. Today was the start of the holidays! I had breakfast. I went to call for my best friend. We played football.

2 When I woke up, the sun was shining through the curtains. I put on jeans and a T-shirt instead of school clothes, because today was the start of the holidays! After I had breakfast, I went to call for my best friend and we played football.

Which story reads better?

Why? _____

Joining words

- Which four words were added to the second story? List them here.

_____   _____   _____   _____

These are *joining words*, which will always make your writing read more smoothly.

What you need to know How to link sentences with joining words to make the writing more fluent.

Where are the joining words?

You can put joining words at the beginning or in the middle of sentences.

- List the four joining words from the story on page 22 under the right headings.

Beginning

_____

_____

Middle

_____

_____

What is a comma?

This is a comma , which marks a pause in a sentence.

- How many commas were added to the second story?

- Read the story again, leaving pauses for the commas. Do the commas help you to make sense of the story?

Taking it further Encourage your child to write a few sentences of a story, using joining words and commas.

Punctuation marks

Meet the family!

You have now met lots of punctuation marks:

- •   I show the end of a sentence.

- !   I tell you to make your voice louder!

- ?   Do you know how to sound like a question?

- ,   I show a pause, in the middle of a sentence.

- Write a sentence using two of these punctuation marks.

_____

_____

Speech marks

Speech marks are the last punctuation marks to meet in this book.
They show where someone is speaking.
"Here I am!" he said.
She said, "Me too!"

- Write a question and answer with speech marks.

_____

_____

What you need to know   How to use commas, full stops, question marks, exclamation marks, and speech marks to punctuate sentences.

Name the family

- Name each piece of punctuation in this story, and say why it is used.

It was hot down on the beach!
"Why not go for a swim?" said Mum.
"No, I'll chase the dog," said the boy.
"Then you'll be so hot you'll need a swim after!" said Mum.

Action reading

- Now read the story and do an action for each punctuation mark.

Comma — at the pauses, bend your knees.

Question mark — at the questions, draw a question mark in the air.

Exclamation mark — at the exclamations, draw an exclamation mark in the air.

Full stop — stamp your foot.

Speech marks — hold your fingers up to look like speech marks.

Taking it further Find examples of punctuation in a children's story book. Talk about why each piece of punctuation is used.

Verb tenses

Past, present, future

We can write about the past, the present, or the future.
The **tense** of the verb shows us when we do things.

In the spring, I planted some seeds.

Now I am watering the seeds.

In the summer, the flowers will open.

Past or present or future?

- Write the verbs from these sentences under the right headings.

Yesterday I went to school.

Now I am feeling tired.

Tonight I will sleep well.

I talked all day long.

I want to go to sleep.

I am going to get up late tomorrow.

Past tense	Present tense	Future tense

What you need to know How to write verbs in different tenses, to show when things happen.

Different ways of writing tenses

- Look back at the tenses you filled in on page 26. You will see there were two different ways of writing the tenses.
- Write more examples below.

Past	Present	Future

Changing tenses

- Rewrite these sentences in the past tense.

I am planting seeds.

_____

I want them to grow.

_____

- Rewrite these sentences in the future tense.

I am watering my plants.

_____

The flowers are opening.

_____

Taking it further Write a story together, encouraging your child to work out which tenses you need for the verbs.

Reading non-fiction

- Read this page of information.

Minibeasts and Messages

Introduction

Insects cannot talk to each other like we can, but they can send messages. This fact page looks at how bees send messages to each other.

How bees send messages

When a bee finds a flower, she flies back to her **hive** to tell the other bees where to find the food. If the food is not very far away, the bee does a dance in the shape of a circle. It is called a round dance.

The round dance tells the bees that the food is near to the hive.

Glossary
hive: The home of a group of bees.

What you need to know How to read non-fiction, and answer comprehension questions on its special features.

Comprehension questions

1. What is the title of the text on page 28?

_____

2. What does the introduction tell you?

   what the page is about ☐

   where to find out more ☐

   how non-fiction is different from fiction ☐

3. Find the caption to the diagram.
   What is a caption for?

   _____

4. Find the glossary.
   What is a glossary for?

   _____

   How do you know which words will be in the glossary?

   _____

Taking it further Find easy information pages in magazines or the children's sections of newspapers, and together work out what makes them different from fictional stories.

Reading log

What do you read?

You read lots of things during the day – cereal packets, websites, letters.

- Write down everything you read in one day!

Day	Time of day	What I read	How long	Author

What you need to know How to read all kinds of material, not just books.

My best read

What was your best book ever? Was it fiction or non-fiction?

- Fill in this description, and think who you would recommend the book to!

Title _____

Author _____

I liked it because _____

_____

_____

I would recommend it to _____

What I want to read next _____

Taking it further In your local library, find more books that are similar to, or completely different from, your child's favourite books. Get together a group of their friends into a little reading group, to say what they thought of their favourite books.

Answers

Page 4
Practise the alphabet
Check your child's handwriting.

Practise joins
Check your child's handwriting.

Page 5
Alphabet sentence
Check that your child's sentence includes every letter of the alphabet.

Why does it matter?
Check your child's answers, and talk to them about their handwriting skills.

Page 6
Long o sounds
b**oa**t, t**oe**, p**oi**nt, m**oo**n
m**ou**se, h**or**se, **ow**l, b**oy**

How do you say ow?

ow as in owl	ow as in crow
cow	window
down	snow
flower	blow

Page 7
Long e sounds
tr**ee**, gr**ee**n
s**ee**, s**ee**, s**ea**
b**ee**, b**ea**ch

Little Jack Horner
H**or**ner
c**or**ner
eating, ch**ee**se
w**ee**, m**ou**se
out, h**ou**se
thr**ow**
pl**ea**se

Page 8
Use your magic wand!
p**i**n, p**ine**, r**o**b, r**obe**
c**u**b, c**ube**, sp**i**n, sp**ine**

Page 9
More pairs
You wear a **hat** on your head.
I love beans but I **hate** peas!
I hope I **win** the race.
Dad bought a bottle of **wine**.
You get ice cream in a **tub**.
You get toothpaste in a **tube**.

Page 10
Endings with -le
cand**le**, pudd**le**, jugg**le**, need**le**
tab**le**, bott**le**, scribb**le**, ank**le**

Endings with -al

animal   petal   hospital

Page 11
Endings with -ve
ca**ve**, hi**ve**
sa**ve**, glo**ve**

Find the -ve words
have, live, slave, give, leave, move, love, Dave

Page 12
Adding -ing
walk**ing**, draw**ing**, watch**ing**, lift**ing**

Drop e and add -ing
mak**ing**, tak**ing**, com**ing**, liv**ing**
hav**ing**, us**ing**, writ**ing**, excit**ing**

Page 13
Adding -ed
talk**ed**, pull**ed**, climb**ed**, listen**ed**

Present or past?
Now I am **brushing** my teeth.
In the past, I **brushed** my teeth.
In the past, I **watched** TV.
Now I am **watching** TV.

Page 14
Hear or here?
Can you **hear** the radio?
Come over **here**!
I can't **hear** what you're saying.
Where's my bag? **Here** it is!

There or their?
I live over **there**.
The twins put **their** toys away.
We played at **their** house all day.
There is nobody here.

Page 15
To, two, too?
It was **too** cold **to** go out.
The little girl is **two** years old.
We're going **to** a party.
Do you want **to** come **too**?

Off or of?
I jumped **off** the wall.
Would you like a drink **of** lemonade?
We saw the King **of** Spain.
We turned the light **off**.

Page 16
Football and superstore
grandfather, newspaper, lighthouse, toothbrush

Thereabouts
every + where, some + times, grass + hopper, there + abouts

Page 17
Roots and endings
draw + ing, speak + ing, explain + ed, learn + ed

Other endings
sing + er, act + or, yellow + ish, lion + ess
-er/-or ending – added to a verb to show the person doing the action.
-ish ending – added to an adjective to mean quite or fairly.
-ess ending – added to a noun to make feminine.

Page 18
Same or different?
Check your child's adjectives and opposites.

Page 19
Adjectives and nouns

Adjectives	Nouns
glittering	sword
gloomy	monster
terrified	cave
fearless	princess

Write a story
The fierce monster jumped up at the **princess**, so she took out her **glittering sword** and waved it at him. With a cry of fear, the **terrified monster** turned and fled into his **gloomy cave**.

Page 20
Punctuation
The seagull flew high in the sky.
It was making a screeching sound.
It then dived into the sea.

Page 21
Is there a verb?

Sentences (include verbs)	Not sentences (no verbs)
My name is Monty.	a big red ball
The donkey ate a carrot.	very slowly
The sun shines in summer.	blue sky the beach sea